So You Dare TO DREAM

ARTHUR MCKAY

SCRIPTOR HOUSE
The Epitome of Greatness

Scriptor House LLC

2810 N Church St Wilmington, Delaware, 19802

www.scriptorhouse.com

Phone: +1302-205-2043

Published by Scriptor House LLC

Paperback ISBN: 979-8-88692-168-7

eBook ISBN: 979-8-88692-169-4

Hardback ISBN: 979-8-88692-268-4

So
You DARE to
DREAM!

Poetry to ignite the dreamer
In YOU!

DEDICATED TO THE MOST HARD-WORKING PEOPLE I KNOW, MY PARENTS' WHO ARE NO LONGER LIVING BUT FOREVER LIVE ON IN MY HEART AND SPIRIT. THEY SAID TO ME, **"ANYTHING IS POSSIBLE."**

LENA DANIELS *(Nana)* and ROGER MCKAY
ALL THE LOVE…

A Special Dedication:

Do You Dare to Dream is dedicated to my first partner in poetry, **Cynthia Elaine Dorsey-Burt.** Thank you, Cynthia, for being there for me during my family's most tragic time. It was you who helped me to turn to poetry to express my grief during this time. Thanks for the many times we shared each other poems. Also, thank you and your Church (22nd) 34th Street Church of God, Pastor Thomas Scott, for publishing many of my poems in your church newsletter. Dorset, this I will never forget. Thank you!

Lots of Love for YOU!

(AL)

Table of Contents

Preface

"Life is but a dream," went one nursery rhyme.

"I have a dream," said Dr. King.

"I'm dreaming of a white Christmas," sang Bing Crosby.

"To dream the impossible dream," declared The Man from La Mancha.

"I Dream of Jeannie with a light brown hair," &

"Beautiful dreamer, wake unto me," lulled composer Stephen Foster.

These are a few excerpts from various corners of life that we have heard on many occasion, which encourage us to dream. We dream of a happy life, cars, trucks, college, family, careers, jobs, peace, Heaven, riches, and fame, to name a few. Dreams are those things we want, hope, desire, need, wish, and sometimes lust for. It is something we do not have in our possession yet. We lay awake wondering and pondering (daydreaming) those things we have yet to fulfill. And when we fall asleep, those dreams appear and seem so vividly real to us. We awake smiling, crying, and sometimes drenched in a cold sweat of the reality of the dream that had us a slumber.

These dreams guide our lives, family, education, careers, and, often, our world. Our goals come into reality through our talents, gifts, and skills. Every

good and perfect gift comes from God above. God has given men dream
and visions to facilitate His will and glory upon the earth.

So, anticipate to motivate your **DREAM** and escalate to captivate the schem
Now, demonstrate to cultivate your **DREAM**, then at the end, celebrate t
begin **DREAMING** again. We need your **DREAMS** to make it through thos
complex and challenging times because they inspire us to **DREAM** too!

Everyone has a Dream

It's a Hope

A Desire

A Must

A Want

A Plan

A Wish

A Need

A Difference

A Light

A Beam

A Gleam

*And sometimes ... **A Scream!***

*DREAMS ARE THAT SPECIAL PART OF
YOU THAT MAKES YOU SPECIAL!*

TURN TO THE NEXT PAGE ONLY!

IF YOU DARE TO DREAM...

... go ahead ... **I double-dog dare ya!**

MY HEAD IS IN THIS BOOK

My head is in

This book

I got to get strong

In these words

I got to get hooked

My mind needs

To grow

And prepare my heart to win

It's gonna take away a lot of my playing time

And hanging out with my friends

I got to get this under my feet

My dream is on the line

I can stand the heat

It's ringing in my soul

My Plans

My Desire

My Passion and

My Goal

The time has come

To make some moves

And take some steps

Don't want to say my dream might come true

Maybe ... Perhaps

Must keep

Reading

Studying

And

Achieving

Can't spend my life

With my head hanging down and grieving

Need to figure out

The Plan

The Plot

The Formula and

The Reason

I am

Keeping my dream alive

Cause... there is no off-season !

DREAM HOUSE

Mom and Dad

Holding each other's hands

Brother and me

Playing in the sand

Spot chewing on his dog bone

Candy and cookies... Ice cream cone

Rooms

Filled with laughter and care

Love surrounds me

Everywhere.

LITTLE BOYS' DREAMS

Little boys don't dream of reading big books

They dream of frogs and snails... not big on puppy
dogs' tails.

They dream of running and jumping

Then spinning around and around

Going to the circus and playing with the clowns.

Collecting bugs and marbles,

 climbing trees,

Running, and jumping in a pile of raked leaves.

Eating cotton candy,

A nd riding as cowboys on a broomstick pony,

Playing on the monkey bars

Pretending to be creatures from the planet Mars.

Little boys dream of being like their big, strong Dad

while waiting for Mom to read them stories in bed.

They like throwing and kicking big, oversized balls,

Picking up sticks, banging on cans,

And tying towels around their neck as Superman.

What happened to those little boys' dreams?

They are not the same ... so it seems.

NIGHT TIME BEDTIME

Praise and Thanksgiving for mercy protection,

Grace and Glory— a time of reflection.

Not merely for sleeping, but

Preparing for teaching and preaching.

Not just for comfort and rest, but

For concerns and issues,

Pounding in my chest.

Not to conclude the day

But to reconcile worries

As I humbly pray.

A time for Dreaming

Without the screaming

Nighttime,

Bedtime

A great place to be

Soul resting easy

With hopes of awakening to Thee.

15

VISION

My mind
Is openly renewed
And expanded to thee.

My heart
Is moved and touched,
A change to be.

My soul
Is swimming in the spirit,
Restless and free.

I can see the Glory in it all
Giving in love by the
Savior's call.

Teaching,
Preaching,
Reaching
For that lone lost soul.

Men,

Women,

Boys, and Girls

In search of Heaven's goal.

Sharing and worshipping God

In honor and adoration.

Glorifying His Magnification,

A plan arising

And working in hand.

A vision of the Kingdom

On Earth

As the Master Plan.

A vision of decision

Not made by

Myth or religion.

NIGHT AROUND ME

It is night around me.

As the sun shines high and bright,

I stand in the dark

With no strength or might.

The cold dark winds

Smother the beam.

My soul is hollow yet, fearful with screams.

Swallowed up in the midnight dew.

A heart covered with black

That once was blue

Drowning

By the smut, crusted coal

That is burning my

Downtrodden soul.

Ashes of soot to trail path, my way.
No glimpse,

No sparks

 Of a bright approaching day.

Sounds in darkness

Piercing my ears.

No whispering chatters of birds lingering near.

Darkness, night surrounding me,

Pinned up against this wall.

No matter where I turn,

I constantly fall.

How can I be right?

How can I be sure?

How can I penetrate this light

To rescue my soul once pure?

My mind has flipped

Upside down.

My heart is

In a tilt-and-spin.

I cannot

Feel my flesh

With so much rage brewing within.

It's cold in here,

In this vacuumed empty shell.

It's a haunted place

Where nothing can dwell.

No sun to warm

My shivering chills.

The moonbeam glows

No illumination

Upon my scared, befuddled brow.

It's night all around me,

Consuming me to be free

In the earth's dark pit, pool of clay.

My fears have been thawed

Into a thick gunk like black molasses

Crusting my eyes in tears.

Oh, Lord!

Help me

Get out of here.

I need to reclaim, reclaim my fears,

I try to push…

But I am pulled back in.

For my feet are shackled

With grit and dirt,

And muddy sin

needs a yoke

To hold on to.

Somebody,

Help me,

Evoke

and drop

Down a ladder of hope.

Oh, God!

Don't you HEAR ME?

Don't YOU CARE?

Ashes of soot to trail path, my way.

No glimpse,

No sparks

Of a bright approaching day.

For my life is lifeless,

With no rhyme or reason

Nowhere to lay my head

No place to rest in bed.

Drowning

By the smut, crusted coal

That is burning my

Downtrodden soul.

Ashes of soot to trail path, my way.

No glimpse,

No sparks

Of a bright approaching day.

It is night around me

As the sun... the SON... shines high and bright,

I will move into this dark

Until I ... find my plight.

A FOOL FOR YA!

Oh yes, that's what they say about me

Believing in something they say it just can't be

They laugh at me saying "He thinks he can walk on the

waters of the ocean, bay, and sea."

Maybe I give too much and strive to please

That thing,

That voice,

That ringing ... that pulls strings

A Fool for Ya!

This was given to me to trek and trod

To stream and scheme

To find the ways and means

To make a difference in the world

To do this and state my claim

Regardless of what people may

Say,

Think, or

Do

I will be a fool for you!

You are my radiant beam

My hopes. My desire. My God-given Dream.

Yes, I am a fool for ya!

OVER THE RAINBOW

Over the rainbow

Where the gentle

Waters flow

People, walk hand in hand

Singing and dancing

Behind a marching band

You will find riches untold

That will fill both

Your heart and your soul

There lies true rest

From your troubled mind

A place of comfort

Simple and kind

Over the rainbow

Where hope survives

And joy resides.

PEPPERMINT CANDY

Red and white peppermint candy

Bubble gum crewing

Yum! Yum!

Butter pecan ice cream

Autumn Breezing in the sun

Shoes with no socks

Walking, I go without destination

No worries nor moments of hesitation

Roaming and soaring free

In my space of no plans

Just being me.

Ice tea, an indulging sensation

Carrot cheesecake

Anticipating a long... long lunch break

The sky is blue

The wind challenges the waves

No wants. No desires. No needs nor craves.

Just dreaming of this special time

When it will be all and completely mine.

A piece of splendor regulates my mind

My heart is in wonder, like a sweet melody,

simple and kind.

WILL YOU MAKE MY DREAMS COME TRUE?

Will you make

My dreams come true?

Magnify my life

Make it brand new

Will you stop

This merry-go-round?

I'm tired of spinning

Around upside down

I want a life

Rich and free

To be all that's inside

of me

Will you make

My dreams come true?

I want to be bold

And reach my

Horizons too

I have dreams
To travel
Near and far
I often look
To the sky
Searching for my shining star

My Goals,
My Desires,
My Wants,
and
My fears
Help me to accomplish
Bring them near

Will YOU ... make
My dreams come
true?

HEY!
You in the mirror
I was told that it's
All up to YOU!

DREAMS THAT DID NOT MAKE IT!

Buried

Hidden

Lost

And forgotten

No wings to soar

No spreading of feathers

No foam that floats

From a creative lather

Pushed under the bed

In boxes behind

That old wooden shed

No notion

To pulling the heart

String into motion

No chills of the winds and waves

Nothing to win

Nothing to save

No will

Lost desires

No burning

Consuming fires

Dreams earthbound

Chained you see

No commotion

No striving

For its lifeless

In me

... I want them back ...

Those dreams that guided me

SILLY

CRAZY

FOOLISH

No matter

What they, maybe .

They are MY DREAMS!

And they belong

TO ME !

DREAMS CALLING

Beckon

Summons

Demand speaking

A loud voice with

Distinct utterance

Roaring

Screaming

Yowling whispers

Requisitions turns to solicit requests

Bellows of shouts

Assemble together

Provoking and buzzing

Heart and soul gestures

Luring seductions

Pulling appeals

Harmonic cries of melodies to yield

Commanding performance for special attention

Cited with subpoena orders bidding to come

Convening with cries of freedom

In murmuring whispers

Your ... dreams are calling.

THE PERFECT SLEEP

I was just lying there

Getting plenty of rest

Breathing smooth and

Easy with the rise

Of my chest

My mind was a

Place of a quiet river

And a peaceful brook

My body floats

With the water

No strings no hooks

My toes tingle

From the sweet

Smelling dreams

And the warm fuzzy

Screams

My heart was merry, and laughter

Filled me in

My soul glided

In peace as

Harmony transcends

Winter wonderland

Soothe my feet

Spring shower

Blocked out

The summer's heat

Sleeping the perfect sleep

Then a POEM!

Woke me up !

A PLACE OF FREE!

Where the earth is green,
And the air is sweet.

The sunrays are liquid sunshine
Splattering all over my face.

Somewhere the water is free
And flowing in peace.

Pure sweet love
From a honey bee

The mountains
Embrace the trees
And the limbs
Cleave to the gentle leaves.

Somewhere
Up there,
Out there,
A place OF FREE!

DREAM MERCHANT

You ain't got

No money

Your looks

Are not becoming

You are not bright

At all

And you dare

Dare to dream?

A WORLD OF MY OWN

Where I can grow

In the sunshine

In the rain

Even in the snow?

My reality is real,

Just for me,

No pleading or begging,

Hypocritically.

Completely my own,

No grass or field

For the buffaloes to roam.

I can still be me

And fly high,

High as the sky,

Swimming to the depths of the ocean

With no whim or worry.

Not hesitating commotion.

Soundly and freely

Resting in the gentle breeze.

Oh! Where the peaceful waters sing the news.

No sadness,

No sorrow,

No Monday morning blues.

A wish,

A hope,

A scheme,

An awesome daydream.

Not a house

But a home ... a world of my own

DREAM DROPS

Thoughts Appear

Images Form

Daydream fun,

Dreams have begun

Fantasying, Realizing,

Wishes spring

Hope arises

Strong Desire

Satisfy the fire

Emotionally Felt

Spirituality Melt

Invent the Scheme

Originate, Escalate,

Create the Scene

Contrive Alive

Concoct the Plot

Vision Clear

So close

So near

Mixed with fun time

And play,

Praying without delay

Delights in God's Desire

Dream Drops

set on Fire.

DREAM WORK

Get Up!

Face Up!

Go to school

Don't hang out on the corner

Trying to be cool

Make Up!

Shake Up!

Write it down

Weigh in the tons

Calculate the pounds

Follow the beam

Work the dream

It's been placed

In the pit of your very soul

It's bubbling over

Don't let it freeze cold

Get to your place

In the world

Run the race

Toss and swirl

Twist and turn

Pray and scheme

It's all yours

Don't you feel

The steam

Share It!

Bear It!

Don't you dare

Let no one

Make you forget it

I DREAM IN COLOR

Vivid light

Sky blue

Things I imagine

And want to do

Finger touched

Clear as can be

Bells ringing

Pleasantly

I DREAM IN COLOR!

It's not a black-and-white world

Possibilities are reality

Rainbow colors

Spinning

Tossing

And swirling

Finger paint

Pastel

Bright

To see

Maple

Apple

Orange

Tall, tall trees

Oh, yes!

I DREAM IN COLOR!

Something

I can feel

Taste and smell

Life's colors

Surrounding me

Life's extravagant

Wishing well

Yes, yes!

I DREAM IN COLOR!

Bright

Vivid

Gold

BIG and BOLD!

Maple

Apple

Orange

Tall, tall trees

DON'T LET ANYONE TALK YOU OUT OF YOUR DREAM!

You ain't no good!

You can't do that!

You are not smart enough

You are too tall and clumsy

You are short and fat

Honey! You can't do that!

You will never be anything !

Girl, you are just like your mama!

Nobody in this family

Amount to anything

And you think you can?

It's not in your blood.

You are too poor and black!

You are dump and stupid!

You'll never make it

So just turn on back!

You are too old

You can't manage the

Rain, sleet, or cold!

You don't know enough

It's too late for you

You must believe

In miracles

Baby, you will be one

In a million.

You stand no chance

You don't even have

a s helter or pavilion

Don't even waste your time

You don't have what it takes

Unless you commit some crime

It's not in your blood to do that.

You are not that good-looking !

You won't make it

You can't break the curse

So just accept it.

You think that's

What you want to do

Boy, your daddy did no good

And we have no expectations of you!

You are a little slow

For that position

Nobody will hire you!

You'll not be one of the proud

Not one of the few.

You want to go to college

And further your education

Who do you think you are?

Just forget it... you won't

Make it that far.

*DON'T LET ANYONE TALK YOU OUT OF YOUR
DREAM ... OUT OF YOUR MISSION*

DON'T GIVE IN TO THAT KIND OF SUBMISSION !

DREAM SLACKING

Don't down me

Don't pound me

Because I have

Dreams of liberty

Dreams of free

Yes, I am marching onward

To reach my higher call

These dreams have captured me

I will stand

I will not bend

I won't fall

You lack the action, motivation, and drive

It's my dreams

That keeps me alive

Don't discourage or try to interrupt

My gain

You have no

Goals nor dreams

That's your shame

You have been given

A mission

A purpose

A life as a conqueror

It's embedded in your soul

To win

To gain

To honor

Don't stay slack

In striving towards your dream

It's real

It's yours

You know what I mean!

Dreams you are lacking

Because YOU are ... dream-slacking !

COLLARD GREENS DREAMS

Mama plants in her garden

Covered with God's green earth

Water and nurtured by Heaven's Sunlight

And morning clouds that bring the summer showers.

Collard green seeds

Collard green seeds, carefully, planted

In the belly of the Earth's core.

As it grows towards the tip of the tilted soil

Released from the ground

That kept it nurtured and safe

It's now mature enough to sprout to the surface

It begins its peep from the Earth

To view the bright rays of the Sun

Viewing the massive sky and space

Of unlimited opportunities.

It smiles and grows fast and better

With eyes opened and arms stretched out wide

It begins to dream of the delight it will bring to all.

It's harvest time

As mama plucks it from the fertile ground

Cuts up them greens, washes and cleans

The pure stream from mama's pot on top of the stove

The savoring of black pepper

Neck bone

Han hock

Or maybe turkey wings

A tap of vinegar

Seasons of salt and spices

Or maybe a bay leaf

It's sensation and aroma salivate

As it activates our

Digestive secretions

Such is a dream planted from Mother Earth at birth

A dream that nurtured unaware, it seems

As we grow in knowledge, skills, talents, and means

We discover

That niche

That itch

That thing that makes sense and clicks.

Our imagination becomes consistent with passion.

That drives our heart, mind, and soul...

Then leads to action

We begin to dream with steam and explode radiantly

Nothing can stop us from striving towards that beam

It emanates from our heads and brightens

The spark that shines from our eyes

We eat it

We sleep it

We dare not breach it

Studying the course and running the race

We don't take our time or slow down

But pursue at a consistent pace

Because we know the dream, we will embrace

Until we get there

We continue the chase

With the cornbread

Macaroni and cheese

A slice of sweet potato pie

And a big bowl of mama's

Freshly cooked COLLARD GREENS

That IGNITES our DREAMS!

GO AHEAD...
I DOUBLE DOG DARE YA!

I double-dog dare ya!

To be more than a thug

Or a post office wall mug

To have a life of hope

To seek education beyond

The normal scope

To challenge the magic, the passion

That's flowing from inside your heart

To strive for more than just hanging out

In the parkway after dark

... I Double- Dog Dare Ya!

To be creative with your time

*Instead of plotting and scheming planning your
next big crime*

To believe you are here in life for a reason

*Rather than standing in the cold snow with no jacket or
coat just freezing*

To believe in yourself and put those

I can't! I don't! I won't be on the shelf

... I Double- Dog Dare Ya!

To take this advice

It will cost you no money

Dime, nickel, or a big quarter

Just a will to sacrifice

To be more than you are

And trust it to take you far

To make your dream come alive

Don't let anything or anyone stop you, block you

Or deprive you...

So strive, contrive, and dive to make your dream survive...

Go ahead... I Double- Dog Dare Ya!

DREAMS ARE MADE OF...

Guts

Heart

and

Praise

Deeds

Glory

Fighting for days

Desires

Spirit

Goals

Soul

Rights

Being brave, tough, and bold

Will

Drive

Steam

Thirst of wonder, win, and gain

Action

Love

A dove with a dry leaf after the pouring rain...

WAREHOUSES FULL OF DREAMS

Cardboard ...

Slabs of wooden crates

Shoebox

Roped, strings of yarn

Masking tape.

Tried and choke

Rolls in order

Not an ounce of hope

Long forgotten

A thing of the past

They came so quick

And time prevailed fast

Teacher

Preacher

A writer of love

Life's upsides and downs

Torn

My wish

My dream

So, it seen

Scatter and broken

My dreams

My means

Where did they go?

Where did they store them?

Standing on the stage

Profoundly renowned

Literature it took

Volumes, volumes

Of pamphlets

And books

Swimming in the deep

Flying in the high

Fears conquered

No more to sky

Reaching the nation

The world

Those needs

Building a family

Taking the lead

Traveling in places

The Moon

The shore

The shining seas

Mountains

Valleys

Snow slopes

Romancing in the wind

Those enchanting notes

Warehouse full of dreams

My whole life

Purpose and scheme.

Trapped in a ... WAREHOUSE

full of dreams.

IT HAPPENED BECAUSE OF A DREAM

The cluster sparking

Chandelier

The alluring frequent

Of a seductive perfume

Planes flying high

To the top of the clouds

Ocean liner

Cruise ship

Little girls

Hula-hoops

Bouncing off their hips

House full of rooms

Saturday morning thrills

Of Bugs Bunny cartoons

The fashion fairs

Flares of brown

Turquoise blue

Diamond cut

Stones

Communication satellites

Mobile cellular phones.

Jacuzzi

Relaxing in a

Room of stream

It happened

It can happen again

All it takes is

Your dream.

MY AMERICAN STREET DREAMS

Hustling

Bustling

Trying to pay my dues

Working hard for the money

To buy my baby some shoes

It may sound mean

So, it seen

Sometimes, I have to yell,

Holler, and scream.

To reach my dream

On the street

In the heat

Making the rhythm

Riding the beat

I have to make

Some deal ...

In making,

The stream

The beam

On the street,

The American dream

Trying to be honest and pure

Working and working

Time to endure

Watches

Socks

Belts

And shoes

Thank you, please!

Hey! Don't you need it?

Selling dope and coke

Hands tied with a tightrope

Yes, I am on the street

With schemes of means

Trying to make

My dreams

I am in it with you

You hold it in your hands

The red, white, and blue

Yes, I want it ...

I want it too

So, I beat the heat

And walk the streets

I work the pavement

To make the payment

With sweat and tears

The day

The weeks

The months

Have run into years

So, it seems...

It's My American...

My American Street Dream!

DREAM DISASTER

My Dream

My time

My mind

With me all the time

The work

The sweat

The tears

Brought them close

Brought them near

I got the fame

I got the game

Anything I want

Solid gold chain

Dreams are real

They do come true

But where is the happiness?

Why is my soul blue?

I got everything

I need in my life

I worked hard

I made the

Sacrifice

I won the race

No more hunt... no more chase

You see I forgot

To care

To Love

To give

To Share

My family

My friends...

I forgot how they supported me

Always being there

Teaching me how

God lives within me

And everywhere

Now, here I stand

With a hand full of Dreams

Alone

...with no one to share.

DREAMS AND FANTASIES

Dreams and Fantasies

Are one and the same

Some shout

Some proclaim

One is a must

One you don't dare trust

One is from the mind

The other springs from

Your heart and soul

Staying fresh and never old

One is wild

Wonderful and free

The other is intimate

And special

Never ceases to be

One is full of life and surprise

The other keeps you striving alive

One reign in true
That other one
Can make you blue

One is simply
A way of escape

One is embedded
In your heart
And no one can take

One will cause you
To sit around and ponder

One will make you
Move and work
With no time to sleep,
Slumber, or wander

They both have their place
And in our lives
And absorbs space

Dreams and Fantasies

Are one and the same

One has magic

One has games

One gives you direction and aim

The other you

Definitely needs to be tame

One will comfort

Your mind and heart

With rest

The other can cause pain and

Pressure on your chest

One is temporary

And shout to live

One has power in longevity

That gives, gives, gives

One reaches from Heaven above

Down to your soulful spirit

One flees from the earth

Wanting you to live it.

They both are elements
In our lives, a need to be

Having rhyme and rhythm
That sets us free.

DON'T JUST DREAM

Don't just dream

Move

Groove

Go to school

Get what you need

Educate

Skills

Drills

Chase it like a hammer and saw

Get in shape

On your mark

Get in line

Position your stance

Don't just dream

Escalate

Plan

Schedule the course

Trek the stars

Consider the winning cost

Not the lost

Focus

Bull's eye, the notion

Don't just dream

Share it

Bear it

Set yourself up

To make it

Don't just.... sit there... and dream!

I GOT MY TIE IN MY POCKET

I got my tie in my pocket

The way is clear

Got my tie in my pocket

It's my success gear

I can smell the heat of

My steam

My scheme

My dream

My mind is made up

I've been reading

Planning and designing

Writing the words that move the play

The lyrics of the songs that save the day

On stage, spilling the beams

The spoken words with passion

Now, I know what they mean

Stirring my soul to regulate my mind

My dreams are free...no ropes that bind

I got my tie in my pocket

And my shirt tucked in

Getting ready in position to fight and win

Standing from that fall

No time to murmur or crawl

People say I can make it

And be what I want to be

In the spirit, they see my dream

Even they hear the screams

The time has come to pull my plans from the rear

No baggage

No bumps in the road

What God has given me is real and clear

No time for fright... no time for fear

I got my tie in my pocket

And my spit shine shoes

It's time to walk and move

It's time to rhythm the groove

Learning the lines

Creating the scene

Standing in the wings

Practice in action

Waiting for the curtain to open

For I am the main attraction

I got my tie in my pocket

A fresh crease in my slacks

No looking around nor turning back

My goals and plans are on the move and taking direction

Strategizing my destination, plotting the action

I got my tie in my pocket

My shirt tucked in

My spit shine shoes

And a fresh crease in my slacks

The curtain is open and I won't turn back

I GOT MY TIE IN MY POCKET!

I AM DREAMING

I can see

I can feel

I can hear

I am so there

On the mountain of my dream

A new today

A new way

Dreaming of things different to say

Putting these words into action

Into play

Dreaming of how to make it a better day

Not just for me

But for all who comes my way.

HOW TO MAKE YOUR DREAM COME TRUE ...

IF YOU DON'T DREAM?

It's inside of you

That drive

That force

Steering and stirring

A feeling that is unbelievable ... but true

You have to pull and push

Your mind to stay on track

Don't make time to wander and look back

Do you want it?

Is it a desire?

Or is it a must?

Don't look at the world in front of you

Follow your passion ...

That thrust ... it's the part of you ...

You have to trust

No one can do it for you

You have to do it for yourself

Go get that ladder and take your dream off the shelf

Stand up ... chin up

Don't bow your head down

Give no time to cry

Don't waste time and watch your life go bye-bye

HOW TO MAKE YOUR DREAM COME TRUE ...

IF YOU DON'T DREAM?

YOUR DREAMS

Compose

Create

Elevate

Escalate

But don't... terminate

COMPOSE

CREATE

ELEVATE

go ahead

ESCALATE!

But don't... terminate

... don't... terminate

...your DREAM

NOT ME!

Everyone has Dreams

But life has a way of

Making us forget what they

Are...NOT ME!

Where is my desire

Where are my wants

My consuming fire

I won't let life lick me

I won't let life trick me

I won't let life kick me

I won't stop chasing my dream

No! No!

...NOT ME!

MY DREAM!

I am scared

I am not good enough

No one would dare give to me

No one would trust

I can't do this... but I must

I have been given a lifetime ...but not sure if it's mine

People keep seeking me

Needing me to be

That thing

That person

And sometimes that fling

Should I give in

Shut up

And give up

My needs

My scheme

And forget about me

No!

My dream is starting to

Wake me! Shake me!

In existence its needs to be

It's my Dream!

WHY DID I DREAM THAT DREAM?

Was it the

Watermelon

Hot chili

With the cheese grits with mustard and ketchup?

Was it her whispering in my ear

As sweat dripped down my back?

Maybe I shouldn't have run that traffic light at 80 miles an hour,

Or lying and cheating to defend my power

The sense of peace in the midst of the rain,

Or dreaming when Jesus

Would return again

Now, why did I dream that?

It sure was funny seeing him fall,

Running from that big fat rat

Staying up late that night,

Reading about that airline hijack

Maybe, it was that

Movie last night, of the hero

Climbing mountains,

Dodging bullets,

Or swimming the deepest sea

Why did I dream that dream

Of a hero shining inside me?

Being strong and bold

No mysteries are told

Dark, lonely, and cold

Why did I dream that dream of being

Gray, winkle and ...old?

Was it those collard greens

With hot sauce that caused

A vapor of steam?

Was it that...

That dill pickle and butter pecan ice cream,

Or the orange juice and coffee shake

Swirling inside me?

Why did I wake up shaking in my boots

After running from a moving train

Hearing that whistleblowing ?

Hoot! Hoot!

Why did I dream that dream?

Of bowing down humbly

On my knees, looking in her face

With words of stammering and stuttering,

Asking her to be my bride

Why do I dream these dreams

That touch my very soul

Making my heart

Rattle and shake

While my spirit is consumed

Then evaporate

Why do I wake up with tears in my eyes

At the breaking of an early morning sunrise?

What's in my mind

That had me crying?

Racing races that never end

The wolfman chasing me, again and again.

ooh and gentle fa

My hair falling out

Then growing back with split ends

My wife

My children

The dog

The cat

Waking up

Cold as ice

Hot with sweat

My heart pounding in my chest

Realizing it was only a scheme

From my collections of dreams

Why do you ... Dare to Dream?

WE CAN DREAM

Oh! We can dream

We can think of stuff

Things we want

Things we desire

Not necessarily

A must t

Wishing and wanting

For that dream

To merely appear

It's so close

To our heart harboring

Harboring doubts and fears

We can tell stories

And sometimes lies

That ends in excuses, reasons,

And alibis

Our face can

Light up the sky

Like a radiant beam.

A smile so wide

A sparkling gleam

We can dream dreams

That make you want to

Run,

Jump,

Then scream!

Oh! We can dream

With plans and goals

Money, money,

Money,

And riches,

Riches untold

Yes, we can dream!

Then life happens,

Binding our hands with ropes

Then we fail to cope

So we pass it on

To our children

In schemes of hope

We can really dream!

I could've

I should've

What a place I'll be

If I would've.

Oh Yes, we can dream dreams

So, it seems.

THAT'S NOT MY DREAM

I know you want me

To follow your steps

In being the best

To carry the banner

That family crest

To be

a Doctor,

Lawyer

Society honor status

To think

To feel like you

To be educated

In foreign policies

And cultures too

That's not my scheme,

Reality,

Nor dream.

You want me to be
The talk of the town.
Honors and accolades

Big bands of marching
Parades

To be a strong and forceful
Pillar in the county and state

You are willing to make
This happens
No matter what it takes .

Wanting me married with children
At that certain age.
You are making me crazy,
Driving me in a rage.

You carry in your eyes
That joyful beam
But it's not my dream.

I know you mean well
Your heart is at best
But please take this burden
off my chest.

As hard
As it might seem
Those things you want
Are not my dreams.

The time and money you spent
Trying to create something
That's not Heaven sent.

The plans
The goals
You made for me
Are far from
What I want to be.

Your dreams and decisions
Don't match
My heartfelt
Dreams
...My visions.

IT'S Your Dream...Happy New Year

The rush is over and the day is new

There is a new frontier

ahead of you.

Last year was great and wonderful

You just have to confess

It was a good year. Yes, your best.

You fought hard

And it was rough.

Hey, you made it through

See there, you really are tough.

All that you learned

From the past year's encounters.

The cold, hot , and wet weather

Will help you and someone else

Think better and dream bigger.

It's your time.

It's your space.

It's your dreams

That need to be in place.

You know what?!

God has given it to you

WE really need your DREAM to help us get through.

So, Dream! DREAM!

Dream your DREAMS into steam.

Fire up your heart and mind with the passion that's making you sick.

You sat on it long enough, so get off your butt or do you need a kick.

Stop playing around,

Go ahead and do your thing.

It's not too silly nor unreal to reach.

Now get off the can

And leave that sandy beach.

It's all on you.

It's all in your hand

Take out the pencil and paper,

And strategize your plan.

Keep moving around

There is someone out there

To help you make that "touch down".

Do something every day

Do the research

Make some calls

Walk the pavement

It's going to lead you on your way.

Give your all and all

Remember what God said...

I HAVE GIVEN YOU THE MISSION

I HAVE BLESSED YOU WITH A VISION

GET UP AND GO!

WERE YOU NOT PAYING ATTENTION?

LIFE'S SCHEME

Don't be afraid to be different

Don't be afraid to think bigger

Don't be afraid to just don't know "no more"

Don't be surprised to look into someone else's

space, world, or life and find yourself.

Don't be afraid to travel into the pit of your soul and find
pure black gold.

Never be afraid to talk to God...and don't feel so odd.

It's okay to grow

It's okay to want to feel and steal for more

It's okay sometimes just to...go...go...go!

Don't be afraid to risk, dare, or take a chance

It's in those times you move,

You advance.

Allow yourself to be true

Allow yourself to cry the tears

That rinse your certified soul.

But most of all,

Don't be afraid to dream.

It's the motivation and love

For life's scheme.

OLD FASHION DREAM

Education with no reservation

Increasing knowledge lost time in hesitation

No time to waste or abandon ship

This dream is mine, I can't let it slip

My will

My trills

Planning for that time and place to

relax and chill

Education is the key

To what I'm determined to be.

It won't come from a wish or a hope

I have to take heed

And review my notes

I am free to dream and be what's inside me

God has given me dreams and visions,

Now I must make the decision

The house

The wife

The kids

The sounds of the church bell

Sweet cool pure water

From a country well

Puppy dogs

White picket fence

Feet up high

Windblown sails in my mind

Soaring towards the blue distance sky...

A PLACE OF DREAMS (...that street)

Can you help me

Find that street?

That place

The corner

Where there is

A consistent beat

How far north

Or south should

I go?

I have heard

Of this place

But, where?

I just don't know

It's a place

Where you push and pull,

Motivate and escalate

An awesome place

Simply great

How long will it take

To get there from here?

Am I close?

Am I far?

Am I near?

Destiny's goals and desires

I heard it's a place

Of ecstatic fire

Life is full and free

Peace is there

Joy fills the air

This place...this place

They say it's found

Within

It is where music and melodies move

And transcend

Can you help me

Find that street?

That place

The corner

Where there is

A consistent beat...

SWIMMING UP STREAM

I am wet and cold
From diving in and out again.

The deep end of a cool spring swizzle
springing up warm waves of sweat.

The vast river, ocean, and brook was open and wide
No place safe to run,
No place safe to hide.

My soul is soaked and free, striving and striving
From the bedrock and beyond the sea.

Sprinting and stroking from diving in,
A flight to race with time to win.

Not drowning from the depth of the
Water pressure that tries to swallow me

The belly of the whale

The sting of the ray

The emerging of a jellyfish

The poke of a shark tooth

Nothing can stop me from floating from bay to bay

Then gliding in assurance, I am on my way.

My target is my dream

As I swim and swim

Swimming upstream.

DYING TO MEET YOU

Coming and running

Coming at you

Running at you

Your dream is dying to meet you

It's running towards you

Don't you run from it

Your dream wants you

More than you want it

Trying to get to you

Before you get to it

You're running a "wee" to slow

Your dream is going to run right past you

And burst down the "doe"

Your dream knows what you want

It's been living in your head

... Encouraging you to move forward

Without being afraid

Your dream is coming and running towards you

When it gets there, you'll know actually what to do…

Coming and running

Coming at you

Running at you

It's dying to meet you

It's running towards you

Trying to get to you

Before you get to it.

Are you ready

To move like a locomotive steam,

To catch up with your dream?

Are you prepared

To run up and down

Those stairs?

Cause…

Your dream is dying to meet you there

DREAM DUST

Excitement, vigor, and desire,

Dreams, visions, and goals,

Coming alive

Misty dusty

Powdery blue

Dream dust

Of life plans

Beaming with truth

Musk of dreams

Musk of aroma screams

Sprinkles of possibilities

Descending in my eyes

Illuminating energy

Of dreams to arise

Puffy clouds

Of images seen,

Dream dust drifting

Into sparks that beam

Rainbow of dust

Swirling into world winds

Spinning wheels

In my mind, passionate desire for life

Chances and thrills...

That brings about a warm fuzzy chill.

It's hard not to "SC

PICK UP THE PHONE!

I am not a burglar alarm

Nor a siren alert

No security has been breached,

I am something you long for

Something you can reach

But I am ringing

Ringing loud and clear

No school bells

Telling you to gather

Your books

But I do have something

I have a hook

To grab you and

Shake you up

I have something for you

Your passion

Your desire

I am the bridge from your

Consuming fire

You know me,

Know me well

I have something good for your ear

I just got to tell

No, no I am not gossip

I am not a rumor

I am truth

It's not a prank call

No collector harassment

But something you lone for

but hid in the basement

No burglar alarms

No siren

No security breached

I am something you lone for

Something you can reach

It's me!

Hurry!

Come quick!

Pick up the phone!

It's me!

I'm your

Dream calling...HELLO!

CORNBREAD AND KOOL-AID

A surge of sensation

filled my mind

Not my ABCs

No! Nursery rhymes

It must have been

The Kool-Aid

and cornbread

I ate... late last night

I dreamed things

That blew my mind

And exploded like dynamite

Can't wait to get to bed tonight

That's the first time

A dream

Made me feel

Warm and serene

No ABC's

No, No! Not Nursery rhymes

Got my Kool-Aid

And cornbread

It's close to bedtime.

HEART AWAKE

My heart aches

Shake and awake

From a dream

To the most beautiful

Experience... of being in love

With you.

DAYDREAMING

I feel a rush running deep within

I feel a smile, and then I grin.

Your bright glowing eyes, and how they touch.

Your gentleness encompasses me, how it means so much.

Oh! Yes! I am Daydreaming of you

To kiss your face and feel your warm embrace

It sends an amble of fire

Burning with such sweet desire.

When I Daydream,

I Dream of how our love is so real and supreme

...A love that's strong and true.

Daydreaming

Daydreaming

Daydreaming of YOU!

WOKE UP IN LOVE THIS MORNING

No rhyme or reason

No Saturday night

No sparks, no flames

No midnight flights

No one to cherish

To embrace

Or kiss

No warm touch

Of sensation

No sweet aroma mist

My heart awakes

To a feeling of

Romance and love

So pure and tender

Like a soaring dove

The fragrance of love

Surrounds me

My heart

My soul

So pleasantly

I woke up in love this morning

I can hear the birds singing

And the church bells ringing

Smiling and singing

With love on my mind

With a surge of emotions

Loving and kind

No rhyme or reason

No Saturday night

No sparks, no flames

No midnight flights

No moonbeam gleam ... But a devastating dream.

MOON LIT TREE

Out of a dream

I imagined you to be

Hoping and Praying

For an angel just for me

Those thoughts end

In a daydream

Holding your hand

As we walk downstream

A desire that stirs within

A melody of music now transcends

Cruising down a country road

Our minds at ease

No fear of a heavy load

My heart is open and wandering free

You are in my arms under a moonlit tree

The voyage

The journey

Oh, what a trip!

That ends so sweet

On your tender lips!

SWEET DREAMS

125

Rest ...yes ... rest

Breathe lightly

Lie your head

Upon my chest

Have sweet dreams

And plenty of rest

As you fall asleep

Feel safe and calm

Exhale in the shelter

Of my loving arms

Have sweet dreams

And plenty of rest

Breathe lightly

Lie your head

Upon my chest

DREAMIN' 'Bout YOU AGAIN

Yes, it's me again

Allowing my mind to wander

How sweet it would be

If you were mine

All the days

All the nights

All the time

Oh! What a pleasure

And joy divine

Holding you

Caressing you

In the middle of the night

Until the sun's pale light

The music and laughter

We've made together

With the beat

Of our heart
Pumping like feathers

Dreamin' of you
Being with you
In our secret place

Picnicking in the park
Until close pass dark

Running through the
Tall splendor fields

Where the budding of the flower
Grow and yield

The moon's shadows
Chaperone us
As we stroll in the cool brisk wind

Hearing...
The music and the melodies
Harmonically transcend

Yes, it's me...caught dreamin' about you again.

ONLY IN A DREAM

Only in a Dream

Can I set myself free

Allowing you to know

Every "Art" of me

Only in a Dream

of a shared sacrifice

Can our hearts

Beat as one

Soft and strong

Like an African drum

Only in a Dream

Can our minds

Regulate the same

Knowing each other plans

Knowing each other games

Only in a Dream

Can our spirits unite

Caressing each other

To soaring heights

Only in a Dream

Can we look in each other eyes

And release the splendor

Of a desired surrender

Only in a Dream

Can we scream

Releasing affections

Of exotic screams

Only in a Dream

Can we hold each other close

And tight

Warm and cozy

Under the Sun's moonlight .

Only in a dream

Can I have you

The way I want... to

With every experience

Exciting and new

Only in a Dream

But not in life

Or…

Can we be bold

Crossing that threshold

Of connected souls?

...IT'S Hard NOT TO "SCREAM!"

Just the thought of you sends a

Comfort so supreme

Your presence so close in my mind,

It's hard not to scream.

The sweetness of your soft lips and your

Smooth and gentle face

Oh! How I remember your

Warm embrace

Eyes that sparkle in the day like the star

At night

As you look at me

It floods a feeling

Flowing so right.

For you step out of a dream

Into my heart of reality

And

It's hard not to "SCREAM!"

BASKETBALL DREAM

To Jaden R.

Eyes full of beam

Standing lean and tall

Running and jumping

With hand in ball

Trying to make it to the goal

To score a point

My plans for life

Working hard and strong

A will to sacrifice

Disappointment and fouls

May come some day

But I'll keep

Dribbling on the defense

With the power to forward my way

I can see it coming alive

That's why I work hard

And push with a constant strive

My arms may not be as long as an elephant trunk
But when that path is clear
I'm going for the dunk

Yes, I'm tall and slim
Still, I can't wait to swing and hang on that rim
There, at the center of the court,
Running so fast
I dare not travel or fall
Got to stay focus
To hear the sound of a net ball

Three points
Hook and Jump
Shoots
Stretching and conditioning
It's gonna take a lot

Free throw
Backboard , lay ups
Can't relax or poop
I'm going straight... straight to the hoop

I'm an athlete

From the bay

Heading yes... towards the NBA

SO…YOU DARE…
TO **FALL IN LOVE…**

SHE DIDN'T SAY NOPE!

She never said no

She waited

She wandered and pondered

She stepped back

To watch and see

She wanted to know

If I was real

With sincerity

I waited and wandered

With great anticipation and Hope

I felt this was going to happen

She didn't say yes

And she didn't

Say NOPE!

I NEVER KNEW

I never knew the POWER of Love

Until I fell in Love with you.

I never knew the STRENGTH of Pain

Until I Lost you.

I just…never knew.

I AM OVER YOU

I don't think much about you

My heart has been lifted

And is no longer blue.

The dreams are far and few

Like the emerging of an early morning sunrise

As it melts away the dew.

The crying has stopped

In the middle of the night

I started eating again

 enjoying every bite.

The mention of your name

Doesn't cause my heart to skip a beat

No more warm and fuzzy

Like a summer's night heat.

No trills

No chills

No visions

Of you running through the hills.

There's a song springing in my heart again

A song that is fresh and new

For I am now over ... over you!!

YOU GROOVE ME!

You play with my mind

And tickle my feet.

Make my stomach

Warm and fuzzy

That makes my body leap.

You sway me and woo me

When I try to stand

There are times

I think I am Superman .

You ease my mind

And quiet my nerves

Make me talk and spin

Saying things, I never heard.

You bring out sides of me

That are rarely seen

You keep me on track

Without a holler or scream.

You arrest my heart

And imprison my mind

In a state of execution

That's electrifying and kind.

Yes, you move me,

You groove me,

Your love has definitely schooled me.

THE OTHER DAY

Feeling empty and lost inside

Since your love for me

You say has died

Fallen from the way of a new and

Bright day

My soul is sad and blue

Seems like there is nothing

I can do

Alone,

Misty,

and gray

Can't think or feel

Since

You left the other day

SO…YOU DARE…
TO BE A MAN…

If I'd Be The Man

If I'd be the man,

Then everything's got to be on track.

See. I don't stand to be stabbed in the back.

I got my piece and blade.

Nobody insults my manhood.

If they do, they will be buried in the shade.

If I'd be the man,

I got to be the boss and keep things in place.

Cause nobody's gonna walk by me and laugh in my face.

Look.

I'd be Tarzan

And you'd be Jane.

When I come swinging around, you better jump,

Because it's you I tame.

If I'd be the man,

You can't tell me what to do

Because I wear the pants,

Socks, and shoes.

It has to be my way,

Or for you, the highway

If I'd be the man.

DEEP DOWN IN

Deep down inside the heart of man

Are his dreams and fears,

His secret celebrated cheers.

The tears that were never shed

For his pride he chooses

To show instead.

A need to explode

With scream-like hollers

From today's heavy load.

Feelings that were never expressed

Sulking, sorrows to a state of depression .

Deep down

Are those hidden words,

Fighting for a chance

To be lifted and heard.

A yearning to be free,

Bonded by restrictions

From society.

Deep down within the heart of man

Are his dreams and fears,

His secret celebrated cheers

Yes... His secret celebrated cheers...

CREEPIN'

Lord, forgive these wicked thoughts of mine

That creep in from time to time.

Sitting and plotting on how to get him back

After he has stabbed me in the back

Seeing that sister and lusting within,

How can I meet her and be that friend?

My heart has been toyed picked and played,

Ready to strike anyone that comes in my way

Oh! The jealousy that comes at times

Because he has it, and I'm wishing it were mine

Lord, forgive these wicked thoughts of mine

That creeps in from time to time.

I AM THE MAN

The man,

I am the man

For I have the master plan.

It's in my mind

Then in my hands.

I am the Controller,

Ruler, and King.

You see, my wife and kids,

Know I reign.

I go to work,

and I pay the bills

Then I come home

Kick my feet up, and chill.

God gave me the dominion and power

To rule my house and run it every hour on the hour.

My wife and kids don't talk to me in any kind of way.

I'll put them back in their place

Even if I have to knock them on their face.

You see, I tell them every day

That I am the man.

And I don't play,

I am the man,

I am the man.

A MAN AIN'T SUPPOSED TO CRY

No,

No way!

A man

Ain't supposed to cry

He should stand up straight

Even if he has to die

He should be man enough

To stay out all night

Without explaining to his wife

Because he has the manly right

Now, look a man ain't supposed to cry

Being softy and cushy

Hold back the tears,

Don't be a woozy

Hey, a man is supposed to fight and win.

Dare not lose face

In front of his friends

No man ain't supposed to cry

He must duck and dodge

And lie, lie, lie

When his heart is broken in pieces

With emotional strain

He must stand up tall

Showing no

Injury or pain

Cause a man ain't supposed to cry

He must suck in his gut

And straighten up his tie

There are people

Who are watching him

They seek his way

He cannot break down

But laugh and play

He must stay strong

Even if he has to

Lie and die

Cause ... a man ain't supposed to cry.

IT'S URGENT

Right now, today

Don't laugh nor cry

No time to play

Hurry up

Time won't wait

No time to prime or plant

Just make the call

All it takes is your all in all

You're waiting like a slave for free

Unloose those shackles

And let it be

Come fast and quick,

You're taking your time

And making me sick

Don't move like it's an emergency,

But run speedily

Because it's urgent

You must do this

You can't just let life go by

Don't let it burn inside your heart

You got to give it more

More than a try

It's all your

Hopes

Desires

Wishes

And schemes

It's urgent

It's right now

It's time for your DREAM!

JED...

Push,

Bite, and scratch

It's your dream you need to attack

Get bruised

Get crude

And board line rude

Push hard

Get in that school

Study the rule

Scream wild and loud

Run like you want it

Dance and spin

Flip and split

Don't let the clock

Run you out

Ignore the

Tick... Tick

Pump and prime

Mix and chill

It's your dream you need to fulfill

Put it on your face

And start the chase

From your head to your toes

Follow your dream wherever it flows...

A FEELING OF GOOD

A certainty

A feeling of a connected assurance

A surrender of the hope that's in the air

Actuality of the realization of the things of hope

A comfort, so supreme that embrace your whole self

It's nationwide so you are not alone

Like a federation supporting you

Penetrating your backbone

It's a song within a song that sways the melody

It won't leave you alone

It's something

That's fresh and new

Remodification of your

Whole indignation

It's the pleasant spiritual connection, a transformation of life "right now"

A sensation

A fantasy

A hope

A DREAM!

A feeling of good ...

DREAM MERCHANT... *reprisal*

You ain't got

No money

Your looks

Are not becoming

You are not bright

At all

And you dare ... to dream!

... yeah!

So...
What's YOUR DREAM?

NSPIRING SCRIPTURE FOR THE DREAMER IN YOU!

Seek ye first the Kingdom of God, and His righteousness; all these other things shall be added to you.

Matthews 6:33

If you abide in me, and my word abide in you, ask what you will, and it shall be given unto you.

John 15:7

Delight yourself in the Lord, and he will give you the desires of your heart.

Psalm 37:4

Trust in the Lord with all thine heart; and lean not unto thine own understanding. In all thy ways acknowledge Him, and He shall direct thy paths.

Proverbs 3:5-6

Every good and perfect gift comes from the Lord.

James 1:17

Commit thy works unto the LORD, and thy thoughts shall be established.

Psalm 16:3

God has given me a special gift, and that is why I have something to say to each one of you.

Romans 12:3

Each of you should use whatever gift you have received to serve others, as faithful stewards of God's grace in its various forms .

1 Peter 4:10

INDEX OF PREFACE AUTHORS:

Row, Row, Row Your Boat

Eliphalet Oram Lyte (1842–1913) was an American teacher and author of grammar and composition textbooks.

I Have A Dream

Dr. Martin Luther King Jr. (January 15, 1929– April 4, 1968) was an American Baptist minister and activist who was a leader in the African-American Civil Rights Movement. He is best known for his role in the advancement of civil rights using nonviolent civil disobedience based on his Christian beliefs.

I Dream of Jennie with a Light Brown Hair

Stephen Foster (July 4, 1826– January 13, 1864), known as "the father of American music", was an American songwriter primarily known for his parlor and minstrel music.

White Christmas

Irving Berlin (May 11, 1888 – September 22, 1989) was an American composer and lyricist, widely considered one of the greatest songwriters in American history.

The Impossible Dream

Mitch Leigh (born Irwin Michnick; January 30, 1928– March 16, 2014) was an American musical theater composer and theatrical producer best known for the musical Man of La Mancha.

Beautiful Dreamer

Stephen Foster (July 4, 1826– January 13, 1864), known as " the father of American music" , was an American songwriter primarily known for his parlor and minstrel music.

SPECIAL AND PERSONAL ACKNOWLEDGEMENTS:

Poetry Partners: Cynthia Elaine Dorsey Burt, Lottie Ponder, and

LiFe Malcolm. You guys helped make me be the poet I am today.

Kellie Hicks: YOU are such a blessing to me, and thanks for seeing things in me, I still haven't seen yet... Thanks .

The Family: Thank you for being supporters, performers, and crew members in many of the shows; Cepeda McKay Sr, Jeffery Johnson Sr, Jeffery Johnson Jr., Curt McKay Jr., Cepeda McKay Jr., Rachel McKay, Zackary McKay, Taylor McKay, Vivian McKay, Annie McKay Brown, Tanya McKay Brown.

My Parents: Lena Daniels (Nana), Roger McKay (Dad), and Margaret McKay (Mom); without you, there will be no me physically nor spiritually.

My Pastor: Bishop Dr. Curt L. McKay and First Lady Estelle McKay, you have encouraged and inspired many poems from the preached sermons and the life and love you share and have for each other. I am Praising God for you.

Thank you, GOD, for placing all of the above in my life. Thank you for the opportunities, for opening doors, and for trusting me with this **gift.** THANK YOU, **JESUS!**

Arthur McKay

Contents